Good Neighbours

A practical guide to setting up a village care group

David M Clark

JR

JOSEPH
ROWNTREE
FOUNDATION

Published by
Joseph Rowntree Foundation
The Homestead
40 Water End
York YO3 6LP
Tel: (0904) 629241

ISBN 1 872470 48 3

Illustrations: Sarah McDonald
Design: Peter Adkins Design
Printed in Great Britain by Ryedale Printing Ltd, Kirkbymoorside

Contents

Preface

Everybody needs good neighbours - never more so when life in our village communities is changing so fast.

As country bus services decline and shops, schools and surgeries become fewer and further between, the premium attached to neighbourly help is all too obvious. Who else do we ask to collect the children from school at times of unexpected crisis or drive us into town for a hospital appointment?

Unfortunately, not everyone can rely on family or friends to look after them. Even if they do, there is no guaranteeing that someone will be on hand exactly when the need for help arises.

That is why more and more people who live in villages are organising Good Neighbour schemes: volunteers ready to supply some of the missing links. They provide transport to hospitals and health centres, call regularly on old or lonely people and will baby-sit in an emergency. Many provide a collection service for prescriptions, others offer money advice and help with form-filling. Some run successful lunch clubs and day centres.

Elderly and isolated people are likely to be the biggest beneficiaries from a Good Neighbour scheme. But others, especially parents at home with young children, are bound to find it useful provided the choice of services is kept sensitive to local needs.

Those prepared to volunteer an occasional hour or more of their time can also expect to gain: by meeting new friends and through experiencing the satisfaction and pride that comes from making a special contribution to the life of the village. Experience shows the enthusiasm generated is frequently so infectious that it leads to other activities, all helping to draw the community closer together.

Good Neighbour schemes are a valuable and exciting addition to the rural scene. This guide offers practical advice on how to set up a scheme in your village.

Explanatory note: Many existing schemes call themselves Community Care groups. Recently, however, the term 'community care' has taken on a more specific meaning as a policy for helping old people and those with disabilities to live in the community rather than in residential institutions (see Appendix E).

Village volunteer schemes may well have an active part to play in making community care succeed, but, to avoid confusion, this guide refers to them as **Good Neighbours**.

1
Introduction

Rural needs

Villages give outsiders the impression of being affluent places to live. Many of the residents are relatively well-off. But there are also social needs which are often every bit as pressing as those in towns. It has been estimated, for example, that as many as one in four country dwellers live on or close to the poverty line as defined by the Income Support entitlement rules. Rural deprivation, more hidden than in the towns, is made worse by the relatively high cost of housing and other living expenses. Incomes for those working locally are generally low. And those without access to a car face particular problems as public transport becomes increasingly expensive and limited.

Social service planners have tended to focus attention on towns where the population is more concentrated and it is easier to reach those who need help. They may be too ready to assume that because people in rural areas make less demand on their budgets, the actual needs are less or that relatives and neighbours are somehow providing all the support that is required.

Village problems have become more concentrated as house prices have risen. Young people have been forced to look further afield for a roof over their heads, while the better-off newcomers who replace them are less likely to make use of village shops and services - thus sharpening the spiral of decline.

How Good Neighbours can help

Good Neighbour schemes have a key role to play in village life. That much is obvious from talking to groups that already exist in different parts of the country. The advice contained in this guide draws heavily on their pool of practical experience. It is also based on closer study of the work done by six local groups, selected because they reflect variations in geography, size, social make-up and different types of scheme.

1

Introduction

The projects chosen were in **Ashill**, Norfolk (pop. 1,400); **Bawtry**, South Yorkshire (pop. 2,800); **Bledington**, Gloucestershire (pop. 400); **Church Stretton**, Shropshire (pop. 3,800); **East Meon**, Hampshire (pop. 950) and **Slinfold**, West Sussex (pop. 1,700). A longer description of each village and its scheme can be found in Appendix A, page 33.

Asked the fundamental question "What is it that Good Neighbour groups do?", their answer might run as follows:

● **Transport:** Schemes provide a car service for people to keep appointments with doctors, dentists and hospitals. This will also normally cover help getting to day centres and lunch clubs as well as to the funerals of relatives and close friends.

Clients are usually asked to make requests for transport at least 24 hours in advance. Some groups organise emergency cover for evenings and weekends when there may be no buses.

Ability to assist with shopping trips depends heavily on local circumstances and demands a degree of discretion. Slinfold Help Scheme provide a weekly run to the nearest superstore. Ashill Village Aid, by contrast, make it a condition that trips to the nearest surgery are not combined with shopping. East Meon Community Care Group are likewise anxious not to deflect trade away from the village.

Most schemes either encourage their clients to make a donation or charge them a specified rate. Volunteer drivers are paid a contribution towards their expenses.

● **Visiting:** Church Stretton Community Care Group runs a comprehensive visiting service for those in priority need, such as the over-75s, and for others on request.

The volunteer visitors may do odd jobs such as shopping or changing a light bulb. They can also call on the services of a volunteer handyman. But they do not do jobs like cleaning or washing that are undertaken by Social Services home helps. The main aim is to act as a befriending service.

• **Emergency services:** East Meon offers an emergency support service for people discharged from hospital or who have suffered a recent bereavement. The group has also installed smoke alarms in the homes of most pensioners in the village and helped get old people connected to an emergency telephone helpline.

Volunteers will sit in with children or elderly dependants when the carer is called away in an emergency. They will also escort children to and from school if the parents are ill or otherwise indisposed.

Bawtry Good Neighbours offer an emergency gardening service, while Bledington Care Committee have reached an arrangement with the local plumber, including a rapid response service and help in prioritising call-outs.

When storm damage resulted in the village power supplies being cut off, Slinfold's volunteers organised a hot soup run.

• **Advice, information and counselling:** Several schemes offer help with routine letter-writing and form-filling. Slinfold have had the services of a financial advisor and Church Stretton's organisers have put together an information pack.

Many schemes, nevertheless, consider advice as a job for the Citizens' Advice Bureau - especially where it concerns confidential, personal matters or complicated social security claims.

The groups in Ashill and Bawtry have formed links with with the national organisation CRUSE to provide counselling and support

1

Introduction

for those who have suffered a bereavement.

● **Prescriptions:** East Meon has a daily roster of drivers (average age mid-70s) who collect prescriptions from the dispensing medical practice in a neighbouring village and leave them at the village shop for collection. Bledington distributes prescriptions, redeemed from the nearest pharmacy or dispensing doctor, direct to people's homes.

Slinfold provides a daily door-to-door service. Bawtry has its own pharmacy and health centre, but the Good Neighbours provide a prescription collection service for those who need it.

● **Disability aids:** Bledington operates a lending service, in liaison with Social Services, to villagers who are considering whether a particular aid would be helpful. Those who have a disabled friend or relative coming to stay can also borrow the equipment, most of which has been donated.

● **Day centres and call-in clubs:** An old coal-house on the village green at Ashill has been converted into "The Call-In"; a day centre that is open all day for tea and coffee. It is run by a team of 45 volunteers on a fortnightly rota.

Partly sponsored by Social Services, it hosts two weekly lunch clubs - one for those living on their own and the other for pensioners who find it difficult to get out. Transport is provided by the volunteers.

The Call-In is also used for classes and clubs, including slimming, dressmaking and photography, and an evening set aside for teenagers.

Bledington's lunch club was started by the Care Committee but has since gone independent. The village health clinic ran for several years as a combined day centre and pop-in club, including a health-screening and preventative medicine programme.

Precisely which services are appropriate for a Good Neighbour scheme depends on local circumstances. Even when local needs have been thoroughly researched, not every idea can be guaranteed success. A hairdressing service at the Ashill Call-In Club, for example, failed to gain enough support.

There are many things that groups would be ill-advised to tackle and lines of co-operation with professionals in the caring services need to be carefully defined. The question of what limits should apply is considered on page 29.

That a degree of tact and sensitivity is demanded should not, however, deter anyone from establishing village care services. Their worth has been proved time and again.

1

Introduction

2

Getting started

Who takes the lead?

Anybody can. In all the groups we looked at, the lead was taken by one or two local people who were committed to seeing something set up and had the enthusiasm to make things happen. But whoever it is will also need to show dedication and a degree of diplomacy.

● *At Ashill, the district nurse, Enid Turner, was concerned that retired people who had moved into new housing in the village were lonely and isolated.*

She persuaded 14 volunteers to attend a preliminary discussion which led to an invitation being sent to local organisations. After a second meeting, a leaflet was distributed to every home in the parish to find out what services were most needed and to enlist volunteers. A committee was formed.

● *Meg Bacon had been involved with care groups in Hampshire. But when she moved to a new job as health centre practice nurse at*

Church Stretton in Shropshire she missed the support that a Good Neighbour scheme provides.

In the spring of 1989, she mooted the idea of a volunteer group and sounded out key people on the Old People's

Welfare Committee and other caring organisations. By the autumn, an article had appeared in the parish magazine and a start-up donation of £200 received from the local Ladies' Circle.

A steering committee was formed and carried out a leaflet drop inviting local people to a series of introductory coffee mornings. Fifty volunteers came forward and the scheme's co-ordinators were appointed. The Church Stretton Community Care Group was launched in March 1990 and includes a 24-hour helpline.

Many existing schemes were started because of some particular problem - the threat of a surgery closing or cuts in the bus service. Others were concerned about the isolation suffered by newcomers lacking family ties in their village, especially older people who had moved there in retirement. Invariably villagers acknowledged that a great deal of informal, neighbourly care was already in evidence, but in each case people saw the benefits of a more organised approach.

The first requirement is to talk with other community leaders to get their views and enlist support. Local doctors, nurses, parish councillors, the clergy and other organisations like the W.I. all need to be consulted and may have much to contribute to the scheme, not least their influence with certain sections of the community. They will also help you to pinpoint local needs.

Some people are bound to say, probably quite rightly, that yours is already a caring community. The important thing to stress to them is that a Good Neighbour scheme can activate more volunteers and make even better use of their time and effort. Organisation can ensure that no one who needs help is left out.

Fixing the boundaries

Most schemes work within one parish or community. This not only reflects local loyalties, but also eases the relationship with local government, community organisations and magazines.

Some groups have considered extending their 'area of benefit' but are generally reluctant to do so because of longer journeys and increased administration costs. Expansion may also bring in more clients without greatly increasing the pool of volunteers. Church Stretton is among the exceptions. It is based on the catchment area of a large medical practice and has recruited volunteers and clients over a wide distance.

2

Getting started

Finding help from outside

You are aiming to establish a community-based scheme under local control. But there are people outside the village who can give you useful advice and support. They can often offer experience based on helping other villages through the same processes.

- Make contact with your Rural Community Council. A list of addresses appears in Appendix B on page 36.
- Ask the local Social Services Department if they can send someone to meet you and discuss the scheme. Many will have community liaison social workers; some County and District Councils have community development workers; a few counties have Community Care Advisors whose job it is to help establish Good Neighbour schemes and provide continuing advice. All of these staff are able to offer help and advice to local groups.
- Contact the district Council for Voluntary Service or Volunteer Bureau for advice, if one covers your area.

Identifying needs

You know that there are needs in your community, otherwise you wouldn't have got this far. But you may want to organise a door-to-door survey to consult people further about the kind of services they would most appreciate and use. A leaflet drop is also a good way of appealing for volunteers. Otherwise, you might organise a public meeting or, less formally, a coffee evening. It's important to make sure that the people who may be using the scheme are given a chance to have their say.

Start-up grants

Maintaining your independence need not prevent you from making the most of the various grants that should be available. Approach your Parish Council, Social Services Department and District

Council for assistance with the costs of your initial publicity. In addition to the cash, they may be able to help with the printing.

Bawtry, for example, received a £300 start-up grant from their Parish Council and Slinfold was given £100 by West Sussex Social Services.

The Rural Community Council will probably have a Rural Initiatives Fund which can make modest grants. It's also worth seeing if the district health authority is prepared to help.

Links to schools

The local school may be able to help you with computers, photocopiers, duplicators and even office space. One of Ashill's organisers is the village school secretary and has access to desk-top publishing facilities.

Access to office equipment and other help 'in kind' may also be available from professional people who are interested in the scheme (for example, solicitors and doctors), as well as from your local Council for Voluntary Service.

2

Getting started

3
Getting organised

You need to give serious thought to how your Good Neighbour scheme is organised. Schemes in small villages with relatively few volunteers and services can survive without much formality. But the bigger the group, the greater the need for a clear structure to keep track of things.

Do we need a committee?

Yes. You need officers who can meet to monitor progress and sort out any problems. Some small groups manage with half-yearly meetings, but larger ones need to meet much more regularly, perhaps twice a month. A committee of between three and seven members, including representatives of the scheme's co-ordinators, is a useful size.

Finding people to serve as officers or committee members requires advance planning so that the committee benefits from a mix of experience. You cannot rely on the right people simply drifting into the annual meeting. Church Stretton are fortunate in having a retired social worker, teacher and policeman on their committee, together with a bank manager, nursing sister and a medical secretary.

The different roles and responsibilities could be allocated as follows:

- **Chairman/woman** - general guidance, chairs meetings and helps recruit volunteers.
- **Secretary** - correspondence, agendas, minutes, plus arranging for forms and leaflets to be printed.
- **Treasurer** - income, donations, payments to volunteers, insurance, bank statements, annual accounts and liaison with grant-making bodies.
- **Organiser/Co-ordinator(s)** - taking all referrals to the scheme, keeping up-to-date with details of volunteers and clients, ensuring requests are matched with helpers, spreading the workload evenly among volunteers.

Some posts, such as Secretary and Organiser, can double-up in small communities, but larger groups will need a Vice-chairman/woman and probably several co-ordinators to take care of particular services.

The co-ordinators

Their task of matching requests for help to the right volunteer and organising appropriate rosters is essential. Even the smallest schemes will need two such organisers or, at the very least, some means of providing cover for sickness and holidays.

The large group at Church Stretton has 20 co-ordinators who take it in turns to provide a 24-hour service, handling all queries, including transport calls. An information box, with card-indexed details of all clients and volunteers is passed across to them so they can immediately match-up requests. A day book and diary are also maintained.

A sample of the clear and positive guidelines that Church Stretton provides for its co-ordinators can be found in Appendix C on page 42.

Street representatives

You may think it sensible for volunteers to keep a special eye on elderly or isolated people living near them. In Bledington, each committee member acts as 'steward' for a block of houses, while Ashill has 16 'companions' who visit newcomers in their area and deliver a welcome pack. They are often the contact point for transport requests.

3

Getting organised

The street representative approach does not always work and some groups consider it too formal.

Time limits?

It is never easy to find the right people to serve as committee members and co-ordinators so it is wise to keep a look-out for new faces. One way of encouraging more people to take on these important responsibilities is to put a limit on the time they will be expected to serve. In Ashill it is three years. That way volunteers will not be put off by the fear of getting 'locked in'. It is also a sensible way of allowing them to retire gracefully.

Annual General Meeting

The annual meeting is your chance to tell people what you are doing and take soundings - as well as electing the officers and committee. The meeting should be open to anybody from the community, including clients and their relatives as well as volunteers. Local councillors, clergy, caring organisations, the police and Social Services should also be invited.

Constitutions

Obviously you can get along without a formal constitution, but it may help to agree a statement of aims and objectives along the lines of the model at the back of this guide (Appendix D, page 51). It will help convince people that you are business-like.

You may want to go further and consider seeking charitable status. If you intend occupying offices, it will ensure you maximum rate relief and allows you to benefit from tax relief concessions on donations and legacies. Your Rural Community Council can advise.

Keeping records

No matter how hard you strive to keep things informal, some records are essential. These may include:

- Names and addresses of volunteers.
- Details of clients.
- Expenses claim forms.
- Receipts of payments, donations and grants.

You will also need to open a bank account.

Many groups will have members who own a personal computer/word processor (PCW). They provide a convenient way to store records, sort out finances and edit mailshots. They can even be programmed to match volunteers to clients.

People who do not drive may be very willing to work with computers. One of East Meon's co-ordinators is housebound, but uses a PCW to record details of all the group's casework.

Note, however, that if records with any personal details are to be stored on a computer *you may need to register under the Data Protection Act.* Your Rural Community Council can advise.

3

Getting organised

4
Volunteers

Recruitment

Finding volunteers is important work and a continuous process. Some people are bound to drop out each year, whatever the reason. Experience shows that once a scheme is up and running, helpers are most likely to be signed up as a result of word of mouth or referral by friends. But word of mouth alone may not be enough. Other ways of recruiting volunteers are discussed on page 28.

Most groups have found that volunteers tend to be newcomers to the village and that local people may feel they are already sufficiently involved in informal care of their neighbours. But there is no iron rule; in Ashill, the village-born district nurse has persuaded a good number of long-time residents to offer their services.

Another tendency is for volunteers to be women and aged over 50. But some groups, like Church Stretton, have made a point of also recruiting teenagers from the local community schools.

Asking volunteers to complete a questionnaire enables you to keep records of what they are willing to do and when. The questions asked by Slinfold (Appendix C, page 45) are good examples.

Knowing your volunteers

You and your clients need to be sure that the volunteers sent to help them are trustworthy and reliable. Making sure requires all your tact and discretion; unpaid volunteers may resent the suggestion that they need to be vetted or watched. But some checks are unavoidable.

Volunteers can be asked to supply basic information about themselves by completing a questionnaire. Some schemes also ask would-be helpers to supply the name of a referee who can then be contacted - *this is essential if they are going to be working with children*. Box Colerne Rudloe Link in Wiltshire report that volunteers positively like being asked for references since it shows they are being taken seriously.

References or no, you will need to make an assessment of each volunteer, noting what they want to do and how you can best use them. This assessment may be continued by the organiser/co-ordinator while volunteers settle in and their suitability for particular types or work becomes clear. Many groups do not see the need for referees or a formal interview, yet most think it normal to 'ask around' about potential helpers.

The advice of this guide is that you do better to be open and make it clear that the chat with your chairman or organiser, although relaxed and informal, is part of an assessment. Although they are unpaid, volunteers should approach their task in a professional way.

Client privacy

Volunteers must respect the privacy of their clients at all times. This cannot be emphasised too strongly. Volunteers are bound to learn a lot about people's homes and ailments; this information should never become the subject of village gossip.

Identity cards

Fussy though it may seem in a small community, equipping volunteers with an identity card (with or without a photograph) can help to reassure elderly people that helpers are who they claim to be. The card used by Ashill Village Aid is shown above.

Training

Offering some form of training is becoming more common, and some groups have found it a great incentive when recruiting volunteers.

4

Volunteers

And there is always scope for improving confidence and performance; your group should want to help every member give of their best. There are personal skills, like talking to someone who is hard of hearing, that many would find helpful. Training can also make the task of administering a Good Neighbour scheme a less daunting one.

The Rural Community Council, local college or Volunteer Bureau are likely to run relevant short courses (maybe only half a day). You can also invite outside speakers to talk to your volunteers; for example, a nursing officer might explain ways of helping to lift frail people.

Supporting volunteers

Volunteers must not be taken for granted. You need to keep in touch with them and give plenty of support and encouragement. Co-ordinators have a key role to play here and have a particular responsibility to share any worries or problems that volunteers may have.

Some groups provide written guidelines or supply volunteers with an information pack (see Appendix C for examples of guidelines). Co-ordinators may also keep records to make sure helpers are used regularly, otherwise they may easily lose interest.

Most schemes also arrange social events for their volunteers. Ashill and Church Stretton hold a Christmas lunch party, Slinfold has a twice-yearly garden lunch. Not only do they tell volunteers that their work is appreciated, they also provide a useful opportunity to get some feedback.

5
The clients

Who is in need?

Your scheme will be open to everybody, so there are no hard and fast rules. The most obvious categories will include those who are old, sick or disabled, people who are isolated and those who are living on low incomes or who have no personal transport.

Several schemes try to distinguish between 'need' and 'desire': a trip to the doctor's may be reckoned essential in a way that a shopping trip is not. It is worth bearing in mind, however, that for many people - the elderly as well as young mothers - a lift is more than a means of just getting to the surgery. It may also be the chance to escape any isolation at home and to chat to someone sympathetic.

Each volunteer may have their own ideas about who in the village deserves help. They will sometimes complain of feeling 'put upon'. You may also discover that there are a few unpopular clients whom volunteers are reluctant to help because, for example, they are thought to have relatives who could as easily give them a lift.

Since each scheme will only work with the consent of its volunteers the best thing to do in these circumstances is talk through the issues, possibly at a meeting with other helpers.

Referrals

Individual clients should be encouraged to make their own requests for help. Some groups will accept referrals from the GP and some elderly or frail people will rely on neighbours or relatives to call on their behalf. But it is generally better if doctors, nurses and social workers can persuade their patients and clients to make contact themselves. That way there is least risk of confusion.

Social Services may ask your scheme to make a long-term or permanent commitment to helping one of their clients. It is important in such situations that they work through the co-ordinators. Attempts by social workers to make arrangements with

5

The clients

individual volunteers are likely to cause confusion and could compromise the independence of the group.

Remember, though, that referrals are a two-way process: there will be times when you need to refer clients to Social Services or the Health Service for more specialist help.

'At-risk' registers

You may want to compile a register of residents considered to be specially at risk. East Meon keeps such a list (on two sheets of A4 paper); this records everyone in the village aged over 65 and highlights those who are over 75 or who have a particular disability. The register is updated annually. It does not include date of birth, or any personal details, but it does indicate who uses the group's services and those who have had home alarm systems fitted.

Keeping in touch

Good Neighbour schemes should be locally controlled. But control must rest in the hands of the clients as well as the volunteers. Once the scheme is up and running you will need to know if the services being provided are the ones that people really want. Unfortunately, that is not always easy; clients may be reluctant to sound ungrateful by giving you the candid feedback you require.

Open meetings and social events can help. But it is also worth considering the occasional survey to find out any needs which are not being met. Groups commonly start off with a door-to-door questionnaire, but it may be worth repeating a survey after ten years or so, to check that the scheme is still on course. Apart from helping your scheme to target aid more effectively, a survey can also be useful in persuading bodies

like Health and Social Services that your community needs
greater support.

The electoral register (available at the district council offices,
library or local Post Office) provides a complete list of adults by
address or by name in alphabetical order. It is also worth asking
Social Services or the council planning department for village Census
data; this will show the numbers of households without a car and
where elderly people are living alone.

Another source of ideas is the village or parish appraisal. This is
a confidential survey designed to yield a broad picture of what the
public sees as the strengths and weaknesses of local facilities. When
you know an appraisal is planned, it is worth ensuring the survey
includes relevant questions about transport and welfare needs as well
as people's willingness to assist as 'good neighbours'. Your Rural
Community Council can advise on both the survey questions and
how to interpret the results.

Ashill Village Aid began with a survey in 1978. This was
followed-up in 1983 with a more elaborate household survey to
which 41 per cent of those approached responded. Most of the major
needs highlighted by the survey have been tackled in the ensuing
eight years.

Service needed	% wanting	progress
lunch club	11%	set up.
meals-on-wheels	5%	set up.
prescription collection	35%	set up (but not well-used).
branch survey	81%	GPs unable to respond. AVA runs car service to town surgeries.
Call-In centre	23%	set up.
chiropody	38%	chiropodists not willing to visit village. AVA runs car service to town.

5

The clients

6
Finance

Expenditure

From the start, your Good Neighbour scheme is going to need a treasurer and a bank account. The main costs that your scheme must expect to incur are:

● **Expenses:** Volunteers are giving their time freely, but that does not mean they should be out of pocket. Drivers should be paid a contribution towards their petrol and running costs. Most schemes currently offer between 15p and 25p per mile; the AA estimates that the cost of running a car is much higher and professional bodies usually pay over 30p per mile. But volunteers driving more than 4,000 miles per annum may be liable for income tax on part of their re-imbursement, according to new Inland Revenue rules.

Sometimes, where car schemes get grants from the local authority, the council specifies an appropriate rate of remuneration. These rates are revised regularly.

Some volunteers may not want a contribution. You should try to persuade them to take the money; that is the only way you will get to learn the true running costs of the scheme. They can always pay the cash back as a donation.

Remember that volunteers who refuse expenses may deter others from joining the scheme. In the long run, the group's success may depend on everybody making a claim. An example of a simple expenses form can be found in Appendix C, page 46.

● **Insurance:** *All drivers should advise their insurance company or broker that they are driving for your scheme.* The volunteers' introductory pack could include a standard letter for this purpose - stressing that no element of profit is involved.

But it is also advisable for the group to take out *two* block insurance policies. One should cover your volunteers for public liability and personal accident. The other is to protect drivers against loss of any No Claims Bonus on their motor insurance. Your Rural Community Council can advise.

● **Administration:** Your co-ordinators and treasurer should be reimbursed for the cost of phone calls and postage, including the job of matching clients with volunteers. Some groups pay no more than the cost of a local call, say 4p a time. Others work to a simple tariff of 11p per engagement arranged. Occasional costs to take into account include stationery, duplicating and printing.

Day centres or schemes that are run from office premises will give rise to other, specific, costs including heating, lighting and business rates.

Income

Never rely on one source of income. The more ways you can think of for raising money, the better.

● **Donations:** Some schemes lay down a tariff for particular journeys, but most encourage passengers to make a donation towards transport costs. They can give the money to the driver - in which case it is best to avoid embarrassment by supplying the client with an envelope in which the money can be placed. Although a tariff may be published, everyone can be encouraged to give only what they can.

6

Finance

Slinfold Help Scheme provide a box for donations in the village shop and at their monthly social events.

● **Charging for services:** Nobody expects a care scheme to behave in a commercial way. But it is sometimes appropriate to make a small charge, provided there is flexibility to ensure there is no disadvantage for those who cannot afford to pay. Some schemes make it clear that passengers are expected to pay, albeit at rates significantly less than a taxi would charge.

If you plan to run a day centre or lunch club it would be normal to make a charge, although this will reflect the considerable help given by volunteers. You should also ask Social Services for a grant towards the costs.

● **Grants:** Local authorities should support Good Neighbour schemes in their area. Given their responsibility for delivering 'care in the community' Social Service Departments may decide to give small grants.

County and District Councils should contribute towards transport schemes, gearing their grant to drivers' mileage claims. East Meon Community Care Group, for example, receives £75 a year from Hampshire Social Services towards drivers' expenses and the cost of a No Claims Bonus protection policy.

Several groups have received start-up grants from their Parish Council. But there is no reason why parishes should not make an annual grant using their authority (known as 'Section 137 powers') to spend up to £3.50 per head on anything of benefit to the community.

● **Fund-raising:** Coffee mornings can raise useful sums; people will usually respond to a worthwhile cause that benefits their own village. Slinfold's monthly tea party - complete with raffle, bring-and-buy stalls and lending library - has elevated fund-raising into a valued social event. It yields £520 a year – nearly two-thirds of the group's total income.

At East Meon, the Care Group chairman, who is also chairman of the village Garden Club, has arranged annual open days at local gardens. The £1,400 a year proceeds go to the Village Good Causes Fund from which the Care Group draws significant income.

Bledington, in the Cotswolds, exploits its appeal for tourists with an annual Open Village Day, including farm tours and an art and history exhibition. Part of the proceeds go to the care scheme which also benefits from sale of a village directory, giving the names and telephone numbers of residents.

Balances

The financial aim of most groups is simply to break even. Indeed, the ability to claim grants may depend on having no visible surplus.

Nevertheless, it's wise to keep some cash in hand for emergency use. You may also want to to build up funds for a new project or service. There is no golden rule, but a surplus of three months' running costs is a good target. Slinfold, for example, maintains a balance of £1,100.

6

Finance

Publicity

Publicity is vital. It ensures that would-be clients and volunteers know that Good Neighbours exist. It also helps existing volunteers to feel valued. Instead of just relying on word of mouth, you should consider:

• Door-to-door leafleting - especially when starting-up.

• Posters in church porches, village notice-boards and shop windows.

• Regular newsletters to helpers.

• A column in the parish magazine - be sure that the names and phone numbers of your co-ordinators appear.

• Careful, occasional use of local newspapers and radio.

There are examples of a newsletter, a publicity leaflet and an entry in the parish magazine in Appendix C.

Most groups tend only to go to the local press when there is something special to report. Good publicity will encourage your volunteers, but they may get just as much satisfaction from feedback via the local grapevine.

8

What are the limits?

Success is bound to breed success, increasing the demands made on your group. So how far should you be looking to spread your wings? What are the main pitfalls you should be seeking to avoid?

Expansion

Some groups have taken a firm decision to stay small. East Meon, for example, have decided that their service works most effectively in one village only and that neighbouring parishes would do best to set up their own schemes.

Recruiting and retaining volunteers is never easy and it is important to avoid over-committing those who do come forward, no matter how enthusiastic. Finding successors to key co-ordinators and organisers can be even more difficult. The long-standing schemes have proved that it can be done, but beware the dangers of becoming overstretched.

Demarcation with the professionals

You are not in business to replace home helps, social workers, district nurses and the other statutory services. Your group must recognise that there will be occasions, such as moving people with physical disabilities, when volunteers lack the necessary professional skills.

The other side of the coin is to avoid being 'used' by outside agencies. Accepting grants from the local authorities does not remove your independence, but your credibility in the village may depend on defining the precise relationship with the caring professionals. If you take their money, be clear that the service is under your control.

Bawtry Good Neighbours, for example, have declined a request from Social Services to provide regular transport for clients to a day centre nine miles away in Doncaster. They are unwilling to act as agents for a policy that was none of their making and which could force up their costs. They also fear that if there was a decline in the number of volunteers available, it would fall to them to explain to

8

What are the limits?

old people why the service was being withdrawn.

Ashill receives help from Social Services for its lunch clubs and has used joint funding from the County Council and the health authority to set up its call-in centre.

Accommodating change

Communities are constantly changing and Good Neighbour schemes must expect to change with them. There has to be space for new services to develop and for existing ones to be terminated or hived-off into a separate organisation.

Bledington Care Committee decided to let their housing work go to a new association which has since achieved funding for an eight-unit rural homes project. Church Stretton Community Care Group have started a new support group for carers in their area.

Paying key workers

Is it necessary to consider paying an honorarium to attract co-ordinators and other key volunteers? Ashill considered paying cooks for one of their lunch clubs, but decided it could appear divisive.

There are no easy answers but be aware that this is an issue that your group may eventually have to face.

Smaller communities

Good Neighbour schemes can be highly successful in relatively small villages, as both Bledington and East Meon demonstrate. Schemes in communities of fewer than 500 people may, nevertheless, need to be less formal and structured. Hampshire County Council's care advisors have begun to build a network of 'Village Contacts' in small communities who can arrange short-term, simple neighbour care. In some cases this has led to a fully-fledged care group emerging. Equally, where two or three hamlets exist close to one another, there are examples of successful co-operation between them to provide the necessary structure and workers for a shared Good Neighbour scheme.

9

Conclusion

Good Neighbour schemes bring the community together. They bridge the gap between young and old and between newcomers and the long-established residents in the village.

Care group clients enjoy new social contacts as well as the practical benefit of a lift into town or a hot lunch. Volunteers get personal satisfaction and self-confidence from their work.

But there is no great dividing line between helpers and helped. Those who are volunteers in one context can quite easily become clients in another and *vice versa*.

There can also be a beneficial overlap among village people who are active in several different organisations. The resulting network of contacts helps to uncover new sources of volunteers and other help. We've seen how, in East Meon, the Garden Club funds the Village Good Causes Fund which, in turn, pays for the Lunch Club annual outing.

The stimulating effect that a Good Neighbour group can have on village life is well demonstrated in Bledington where success has coincided with a revival of W.I. activities and growth of a lively local history group. Local mothers have organised a playgroup transport rota, a magazine has been launched by the parish clerk and someone

9

Conclusion

else has started village hall bingo sessions to pay for Christmas baskets for old people.

The evidence from the groups studied is that Good Neighbour schemes work regardless of village size or social mix. There is no doubt that it is easier to get going in villages where a spirit of voluntary action already exists. But even if communities are socially divided or depressed, action is still possible - although a care group may need to be introduced as part of wider community development programme under professional guidance.

The sheer variety of villages where Good Neighbours are now a welcome fact of village life shows that, with suitable adaptation, a scheme can be established in almost any rural community.

Appendix A

Six Good Neighbour Schemes

Existing Good Neighbour schemes tend to be concentrated in the South and East of England. However, the six village groups featured in this guide were chosen to give a geographical spread as well as a selection of sizes and social mix.

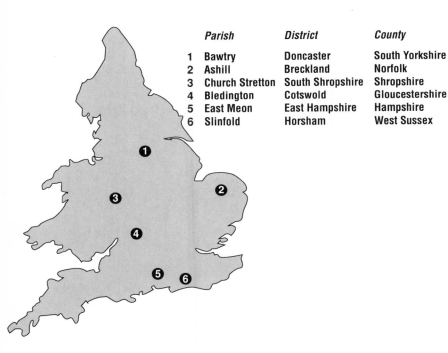

	Parish	District	County
1	Bawtry	Doncaster	South Yorkshire
2	Ashill	Breckland	Norfolk
3	Church Stretton	South Shropshire	Shropshire
4	Bledington	Cotswold	Gloucestershire
5	East Meon	East Hampshire	Hampshire
6	Slinfold	Horsham	West Sussex

1. Bledington Care Committee

Bledington is the smallest community studied for this guide, with a population of 400 at the time of the 1981 Census. It lies in the Cotswolds on the Gloucestershire-Oxfordshire border. Cheltenham and Oxford are 21 miles away but the nearest cottage hospital is closer in Chipping Norton. It is a traditional agricultural settlement with a large number of 'newcomers' in the older cottages and more modern housing. It has serious transport and housing problems.

Bledington Care was set up during the 1973 miners' strike to provide temporary relief during power cuts, but has since become a major force in revitalising village life.

2. East Meon Community Care Group

East Meon is an agricultural village (population 800) nestling in the Hampshire Downs. The village core is inhabited by relatively wealthy newcomers with 'locals' living on the newer council estates on the periphery. The parish population is swollen to 1,560 by a naval establishment, although the village is 20 miles from Portsmouth.

The Care Group was formed in 1985 with outside help from the Diocesan Community Care Advisor who has helped establish several groups in the county. It works to a fairly informal structure providing a range of transport and 'neighbouring' services. It makes the most of other networks in the village that are highly successful in raising funds.

3. Ashill Village Aid

Ashill is a traditional agricultural community in a remote area of Norfolk Breckland, some 20 miles from Norwich and Kings Lynn. Its character has been altered by new housing in the past 20 years which has brought many retired people into the village, notably from London.

It was the problems of adjustment that prompted the district nurse to set up Village Aid in 1977. It provides a range of transport and neighbouring services and has set up its own call-in centre as a venue for lunch clubs, activities and classes.

4. Slinfold Help Scheme

Slinfold is a much-expanded village with a population of 1,700 close to Horsham in West Sussex. It has been affected by the spread of London's commuter belt and gives the impression of being wealthy. There are, nevertheless, a large proportion of pensioners, people in council housing and people with no car. Transport is a particular problem.

Slinfold Help started in 1981. It is organised on a fairly informal basis and provides a wide range of services, including a monthly social event that helps to generate a financial surplus used to fund other local services.

5. Bawtry Good Neighbours

Situated some 9.5 miles from Doncaster, this South Yorkshire village of 2,800 has good public transport facilities by rural standards. There are public services in the village including a health centre, library and a range of shops. The social mix is broad including Doncaster commuters and mine-workers.

Bawtry Good Neighbours was launched in 1984 by a development worker who lived in the village with the help of Doncaster Council for Voluntary Service. There was a need to help isolated members of the community. A range of services is provided; transport - despite the relatively good conventional facilities - is most in demand.

6. Church Stretton Community Care Group

Really a small town in the hill country of South Shropshire, the village has a population of 2,700 and the parish 3,800. Shrewsbury is 12 miles away. The village has a large number of council houses and has also attracted significant numbers of commuters and retired people.

The Community Care Group was started by the practice nurse at the health centre, drawing on her previous experience in Hampshire. It is the only scheme to cover a number of parishes, serving most of the health centre catchment area (pop. 5,800). It has adopted a relatively structured organisation with a large number of volunteers.

Appendix B

Sources of help

Local advice and information. Your county **Rural Community Council** can provide a range of advice and help on organisation, constitution, charity status and insurance. They should be able to send somebody to a meeting, and will already have close contact with your parish council and village hall committee. A list of addresses appears at the end of this appendix.

They will probably administer a small start-up grant scheme (the Rural Initiative Fund). Most publish a magazine and carry a stock of self-help publications from ACRE (Action with Communities in Rural England) and NCVO (National Council for Voluntary Organisations).

The RCC can also put you in touch with the right people in other organisations locally, including:

- The district **Council of Voluntary Service** if one covers your area. This body is likely to be very involved with neighbourhood care issues.
- The county office of **Age Concern.**
- The **Volunteer Bureau** if one covers your area.

The Social Services Department

They will be able to give general advice and help you to establish where the gaps in local services may be. Social Services should be able to offer an initial grant. You may also want to approach the District Health Authority and the District or Borough Council for advice and grant-aid.

National sources of ideas

The **Volunteer Centre** has a range of useful publications on aspects of volunteering. Their address is:

29 Lower King's Road, Berkhamsted, Herts HP4 2AB
Tel: 0442 873311

The Rural Team of the **National Council for Voluntary Organisations** have published *Ways to Care*, a series on how neighbourhood care can work in rural areas, as well as other publications relating to volunteering and neighbourhood care in the rural context.

26 Bedford Square, London WC1B 3HU Tel: 071-636 4066.

Rural Community Councils Address List

(This list was correct at 1 July 1991.)

Avon Community Council
209 Redland Road
Bristol BS6 6YU
Tel: 0272 736822

Bedfordshire Rural Community Council
The Old School
Southill Road
Cardington
Bedford MK44 3SX
Tel: 0234 838771
Fax: 0234 838149

Community Council for Berkshire
Epping House
55 Russell Street
Reading RG1 7XG
Tel: 0734 566556

Buckinghamshire Council for Voluntary Service
Walton House
Walton Street
Aylesbury HP21 7QQ
Tel: 0296 21036

Cambridgeshire Community Council
218 High Street
Cottenham
Cambridge CB4 4RZ
Tel: 0954 50144

Cheshire Community Council
96 Lower Bridge Street
Chester CH1 1RU
Tel: 0244 322188/323602

Cleveland Council for Voluntary Service
47 Princes Road
Middlesborough
Cleveland TS1 4BG
Tel: 0642 240651/2

Appendix B

Sources of help

Cornwall Rural Community Council
9a River Street
Truro TR1 2RS
Tel: 0872 73952

Voluntary Action Cumbria
Birbeck House
Duke Street
Penrith CA11 7NA
Tel: 0768 68086

Derbyshire Rural Community Council
Church Street
Wirksworth
Derby DE4 4EY
Tel: 062982 4797

Community Council for Devon
County Hall
Topsham Road
Exeter EX2 4QD
Tel: 0392 382533/383681
Fax: 0392 411279

Community Council for Dorset
57 High West Street
Dorchester DT1 1UT
Tel: 0305 262270

Durham Rural Community Council
Aykley Heads
Durham DH1 5UN
Tel: 091 384 3511

Rural Community Council of Essex
Mackmurdo House
79 Springfield Road
Chelmsford CM2 6JG
Tel: 0245 352046
Fax: 0245 495427

Gloucestershire Rural Community Council
Community House
15 College Green
Gloucester GL1 2LZ
Tel: 0452 28491

Hampshire Council of Community Service
Beaconsfield House
Andover Road
Winchester SO22 6AT
Tel: 0962 854971
Fax: 0962 841160

Community Council of Hereford & Worcester
Great Malvern Station
Station Approach
Malvern WR14 3AU
Tel: 0684 573334
Fax: 0684 573367

Community Council for Hertfordshire
2 Townsend Avenue
St Albans AL1 3SG
Tel: 0727 52298

Community Council of Humberside
14 Market Place
Howden
Goole DN14 7BJ
Tel: 0430 430904
Fax: 0430 432037

Isle of Wight Rural Community Council
42 The Mall
Carisbrook Road
Newport
Isle of Wight PO30 1BW
Tel: 0983 524058
Fax: 0983 526905

Kent Rural Community Council
15 Manor Road
Folkestone CT20 2AH
Tel: 0303 850816

Community Council of Lancashire
15 Victoria Road
Fulwood
Preston PR2 4PS
Tel: 0772 717461

Leicestershire Rural Community Council
Community House
133 Loughborough
Leicester LE4 5LX
Tel: 0533 662905

Appendix B

Sources of help

Community Council of Lincolnshire
Corn Exchange Chamber
17a Market Place
Sleaford NG34 7SP
Tel: 0529 302466
Fax: 0529 414267

Norfolk Rural Community Council
20 Market Place
Hingham
Norfolk NR9 4AF
Tel: 0953 851408
Fax: 0953 850695

Northamptonshire Rural Community Council
Hunsbury Hill Centre
Harksome Hill
Northampton NN4 9QX
Tel: 0604 765888

Community Council of Northumberland
Tower Buildings
9 Oldgate
Morpeth NE61 1PT
Tel: 0670 517178

Nottinghamshire Rural Community Council
Minster Chambers
Church Street
Southwell NG25 0HD
Tel: 0636 815267

Oxfordshire Rural Community Council
The Hadow Rooms
101 Banbury Road
Oxford OX2 6NE
Tel: 0865 512488

Community Council of Shropshire
1 College Hill
Shrewsbury SY1 1LT
Tel: 0743 360641

Community Council for Somerset
St. Margaret's
Hamilton Road
Taunton TA1 2EG
Tel: 0823 331222/3
Fax: 0823 323652

Sources of help

Community Council of Staffordshire
St. Georges
Corporation Street
Stafford ST16 3AG
Tel: 0785 42525
Fax: 0785 42176

Suffolk/Acre
Alexandra House
Rope Walk
Ipswich IP4 1LZ
Tel: 0473 264595
Fax: 0473 264594

Surrey Voluntary Services Council
Jenner House
2 Jenner Road
Guildford GU1 3PN
Tel: 0483 66072

Sussex Rural Community Council
Sussex House
212 High Street
Lewes BN7 2NH
Tel: 0273 473422
Fax: 0273 483109

Warwickshire Rural Community Council
The Abbotsford
10 Market Place
Warwick CV34 4SL
Tel: 0926 499596

Community Council for Wiltshire
Wyndhams
St Joseph's Place
Bath Road
Devizes SN10 1DD
Tel: 0380 722475

Yorkshire Rural Community Council
William House
Skipton Road
Skelton
York YO3 6XW
Tel: 0904 645271

Appendix C

Sample documents

1. Guideline for Co-ordinators - Church Stretton Community Care Group

On taking a call

1. Always have a pen and paper by the phone and have Care Group Information ready to refer to.

2. Answer "Care Group - Can I help you?" like you really *do* want to help.

3. Repeat and write down name, address and telephone number and get directions (where applicable).

4. If unsure about the suitability of the task we're being asked to do, say you will discuss it with a colleague or the committee and ring them back.

5. Don't be afraid to say NO if it's not our remit. Refer to appropriate agencies, eg Red Cross, GP etc, where necessary.

6. You are a Care Group Representative, so even if unable to do the task asked for, explain what we're about and areas in which we could help. *Always endeavour to leave the Client with a positive feeling about the group.*

2. Guidelines for Co-ordinators on ringing volunteers for help - Church Stretton Community Care Group

- be friendly, cheerful, optimistic, encouraging.
- keep smiling (it is reflected in your voice), unless of course a smile would be quite inappropriate to what you have to say.
- be specific about the task you want done.
- accept a refusal cheerfully (so that you can ask again on another occasion).

DON'T

- be reproachful (even if the excuse is weak).
- be apologetic.
- show your desperation (even when you reach the end of your list).
- put too big a responsibility on the volunteer. (It is the co-ordinator's job to break the request down into manageable tasks.)

- make the volunteer feel guilty. (They may be less willing to offer help another time).
- give the more confidential details about the person until the volunteer has agreed.
- break essential confidences from the client or the referring agency.

When a volunteer has agreed to help

1. Confirm clearly dates, times, name, address, who to contact in case of difficulty.

2. Give any information needed to enable the volunteer to undertake the task properly, if necessary getting agreement to passing on confidential details (eg a driver needs to know of a passenger's disabilities; a visitor to an elderly person needs to know if he/she is confused or at risk of a heart attack; someone giving support to a mother with young children needs to know if she is a single parent).

3. Ask the volunteer to report back to the co-ordinator either on completion or after the first visit, where appropriate.

3. Guidelines for volunteers - Bawtry Good Neighbours

1. Identity Card

Each volunteer has been issued with a yellow identity card. This may appear somewhat official for a Group such as ours but it is important that the public, and especially the elderly, can check that you are a genuine Bawtry Good Neighbour. It would be helpful if you could remember to carry the card with you on Good Neighbour tasks and thereby avoid any embarrassment if asked to show it.

2. Insurance Cover for Volunteer Drivers

It is the volunteer's own responsibility to ensure that he/she is covered by his/her own Insurance Policy for voluntary driving. We suggest you contact your insurance company to inform them that you wish to undertake voluntary driving from time to time for Bawtry Good Neighbours and ask them:

(a) are you covered by your existing policy for voluntary driving?

(b) if not, can your existing policy be extended at no extra charge?

(c) if an additional premium is required, how much will it be?
When you have been through this procedure, could you then please confirm to the Co-ordinator that you are covered.

We hope very much that prospective drivers will not be put off by having to check these points, as voluntary driving is often one of the most frequently used services in a Good Neighbour scheme.

Appendix C

Sample documents

3. Insurance cover for volunteers

Volunteers are fully covered by an appropriate insurance policy while undertaking voluntary duties for Bawtry Good Neighbours.

4. Expenses

All volunteers are entitled to be reimbursed for expenses incurred while on Good Neighbour business, i.e. telephone calls, mileage allowance (currently 10p per mile), parking fees, etc. Relevant details should be set out clearly on an Expenses Claim Form (copy attached) and passed to the Co-ordinator for reimbursement as frequently as you wish. Reimbursement can be in the form of cash or a cheque: a cheque may take a little longer as it requires two signatures.

5. General

As a volunteer you should remember:

- not to over-commit yourself but to keep a balance between voluntary tasks and personal/family commitments
- not to agree to undertake tasks which you are unhappy about
- to be honest. If you are not happy about anything to do with the Group, please feel free to discuss it with the Co-ordinator
- if you are unable to keep to arrangements, tell the appropriate person
- to provide feedback, suggestions and recommendations where necessary
- to inform the Co-ordinator if your availability/preferences change, if you are planning to be away from home for any length of time or if you no longer wish to be involved with the Group
- to refer any potential volunteers, however little they feel they have to offer, to the Co-ordinator
- Inevitably problems will arise, particularly during the first few months. Any feedback, suggestions or recommendations you are able to pass to the Co-ordinator will then be discussed at volunteers meetings or by the Steering Committee if necessary.

4. Volunteer form - Slinfold Help Scheme

Transport (Mileage allowance is payable)
I am prepared to help with:
1. Emergency and/or essential transport.
2. Collect prescriptions.
3. Do shopping.
4. Collect a child from school.

Other forms of help (where a car is not needed)
1. Look after toddlers.
2. Look after or sit with a baby.
3. Collect a child from school.
4. Sit with an elderly person who can't be left alone.
5. Visit and make friends with housebound or lonely people.
6. Give practical advice over finance matters.
7. Walk a dog while owner is ill.
8. Collect shopping lists.

Please say if there is one particular day you go to Crawley, Horsham or Billingshurst.

_____

Please enter the days when you are not available for emergency calls.

_____

Please enter the days when it is not convenient for you to be called on to help.

Name: _____

Address: _____

_____

Post code: _____ Telephone No:_____

Transport
This is the key role of the Help Scheme. We have, in visiting homes in Slinfold, found a great deal of kindhearted and almost devoted neighbourliness, but this does not cancel out the need for cars for surgery visits, visiting to see hospital patients, urgent prescriptions and so on.

Please help us by joining the Help Transport Scheme. It would be wise to check that your insurance covers giving lifts; Comprehensive Policies normally do.

If you have any other suggestions for giving help, please enter them here:

_____

Appendix C

Sample documents

5. Claim for expenses - Slinfold Help Scheme

Name:_____

Address:_____

Date	Client	Service Provided	Car Miles	Other Expenses 'phone/post etc	£ p

Totals_____   £ _____

Mileage due £ _____

£ _____

Received sum of _____

6. Text of Issue No 4 - Bawtry Good Neighbours Newsletter

What is a good neighbours group?

It is a group of Volunteers who have offered to give others in the neighbourhood the kind of informal help a relative or caring neighbour might undertake.

Surely most of us do this anyway!

Yes, of course we do - looking after a neighbour's kids when their Mum is ill, shopping for a friend.

But ...

some people don't have friends or relatives nearby and don't know who to turn to.

Others ...

have a little time to spare and would like to be useful to somebody but are afraid to suggest help.

So...

Bawtry Good Neighbours is a means of linking those needing assistance with those willing to give it.

What kind of help is available?

The aim of the Group is to respond immediately to local need, act in cases of emergency and give support in times of stress. Help will often be of a practical nature on a short-term/emergency basis but for some, especially the lonely or the housebound, longer-term support and care can be offered.

Some ways in which Bawtry Good Neighbours can help

1. Support e.g. for the housebound and disabled and those caring for them; those with young children; befriending; regular visiting; family emergencies and other general support.
2. Transport e.g. emergencies; hospital visits; to the Health Centre; medical appointments, shopping, visiting sick relatives/friends.
3. General e.g. small handyman tasks; local shopping; prescription collecting; collecting library books; help with form-filling and letter writing; general errands and help.

However, these are only a few examples of ways in which the Group might be of assistance. Perhaps a better way of putting it might be:

If you have a request which you would be happy about asking a really good neighbour to do, then do get in touch with us. We will treat your request with confidence.

Bawtry Good Neighbours can put you in touch with other voluntary organisations if you require more specialized help.

OR

do you need to borrow a wheelchair, commode, high chair, cot, etc. for a short time? If so, get in touch with us.

We also have available some special mattresses and cushions. The Community Nurses lend these to people who need them.

What sort of people can be volunteers?

Everybody in the community has something to offer. The good thing is that you can offer as much or as little time as you can spare and you don't need any special skills to be involved. Even if you are housebound, there are many useful ways in which you can help.

Initially there is a form to fill in which will give us an idea of how you would like to help, when you would be available, etc. Then you

Appendix C

Sample documents

will be issued with an Identity Card. This might seem rather official, but it's important that the public have some means of ensuring that you really are a Bawtry Good Neighbour.

Volunteers using their own cars to provide transport are able to claim a mileage allowance and all volunteers are entitled to claim out-of-pocket expenses.

Informal volunteers' get-togethers are held three or four times a year and volunteers are also kept in touch with the Group's activities through a regular newsletter.

New volunteers are always needed. If you would like to know more about becoming a volunteer, please tell a Telephone Contact, who will put you in touch with the Co-ordinator.

Co-ordinator's message

In the 6 years that BGN has been active we have gone from strength to strength. In 1989 we answered over 350 requests for help - that's more than one good turn every day. We have visited the lonely, collected prescriptions, taken housebound people to hospital appointments, helped out during family emergencies, etc., etc.

We are always happy to provide transport for those who genuinely need it, but some people unfortunately still think of us as a cheap taxi service. All our volunteers give freely and willingly of their time and energy; volunteers available to provide transport (especially during the day) are as precious as gold to us, so please do not abuse their services.

We really do need more volunteers (especially ones with transport). If you would like to help, please ring one of the telephone contacts **today**. Almost anyone can be a volunteer: we ask only for your time and your enthusiasm.

Please continue to make good use of us.

Chairman's message

I am very proud of my involvement with BGN. I know most of the volunteers personally and can vouch for the fact that they are genuinely caring people who want to do some good for the less fortunate members of our community. Our volunteers are not snoopers nor gossips and requests for help are private matters.

So if you have a problem and don't know who to turn to for help, try BGN.

Dr E A Burroughs

How to get in touch

First of all, get in touch with any one of the following Telephone Contacts. If you don't get a reply, then try someone else on the list. Each Telephone Contact has details of all the volunteers and will hopefully be able to meet your request.

Please do NOT contact volunteers directly.

Telephone Contacts

Mrs Carol Davis

Mrs Helen Dean

Mrs Freda Layen

Mrs Elizabeth Matthews

Mrs Gillian Platt

We would request that you telephone between 9am and 9pm unless you have a genuine emergency.

Joint Co-ordinators

Mrs Merle Mothersdale and

Mrs Ella Bolland

Remember - each volunteer has been issued with a bright yellow Identity Card with photograph attached. Don't be shy about asking to see it if that person is not already known to you.

Further copies of this leaflet are available from the library or the Health Centre.

7. Insert in parish magazine - East Meon Care Group

Care Group

The group continues to provide transport and we welcome volunteers to help with this work.

If you require transport or any other help please phone one of the co-ordinators:

Mr J Rothwell or Mrs E Spreadbury

It helps if you can give as much notice as possible as the co-ordinators often have to make a number of phone calls to find an available driver.

We still need some more committee members - only four meetings per year - any volunteers please phone

JAP Street, Chairman

Appendix C

Sample documents

8. Door-to-door leaflet - Church Stretton Community Care Group

CHURCH STRETTON COMMUNITY CARE GROUP

Serving: Dorrington, Longnor, Frodesley, Smethcott, Woolstaston, Leebotwood, Plaish, Cardington, Longville, Rushbury, Hope Bowdler, Acton Scott, Minton, Wistanstow, Hatton, Ticklerton, All Stretton, Little Stretton and Church Stretton

Church Stretton Community Care Group exists to help YOU
- During illness
- In an emergency
- As you grow older
- After the arrival of a new baby
- When someone dies
- When someone relies on your constant care
- When things go wrong
- When a child is ill
- At any time

INTERESTED?
Do you need help?
Can you give help?

Ring us on Church Stretton 724242

Appendix D

Model constitution

1. Name The name of the Group shall be ...

2. Aims The object of the Group is to advance any charitable purposes for the benefit of the community of ... , and particularly to provide help in cases of need for the residents of the Parish of ...
The Group shall:
a. raise funds and invite and receive contributions by way of subscription, donation and otherwise
b. recruit suitable volunteers for the furtherance of such aims
c. do all such other lawful things as shall further the objects

3. Membership shall be open to any residents of the Parish of ... who are willing to give their time or resources towards helping those in need and to foster community spirit within parish.

4. The Committee The Group shall be managed by a Committee which shall include a Chairman/woman, Vice-Chairman/woman, Secretary, Organiser, Treasurer plus two other members.

The Committee shall meet not less than three times a year and a formal record of such meetings shall be kept. Four Committee members shall constitute a quorum. The Chairman/woman shall have a second casting vote at meetings of the Committee.

The Chairman/woman, in consultation with any two elected officers, shall be invested with all the powers necessary to secure the efficient day-to-day running of the Group. The Officers shall report on the exercise of such day-to-day powers to the next meeting of the Committee.

5. Annual General Meeting The Annual General Meeting (AGM) shall be held by (date) every year, when a report of the year's activities shall be presented. Any resident of the Parish of ... shall be entitled to attend and vote as shall all volunteers and recipients of services given by the volunteers.

A special meeting shall be convened at the request of two-thirds of the Committee members. Such meetings shall be held within seven days of the request being received by the Secretary.

Appendix D

A model constitution

Nominations for Officers and Committee members shall be made at the Annual General Meeting and will be elected on a show of hands.

The Committee shall have the power to fill any vacancies arising between annual meetings by way of co-option. Such appointments shall service until the next AGM.

Officers may serve for up to three years, after which they must stand down from that post, although they may be appointed to other posts. They may be re-appointed to the same post after a period of two years has elapsed.

6. Volunteers All volunteers will be issued with identity cards which they should carry when acting on behalf of the Group.

7. Finance The Treasurer shall keep an account of all income and expenditure and shall submit accounts, duly audited, at the AGM. There shall be a bank account in the name of the Group on the signature of any two of the Chairman/woman, Secretary or Treasurer. An Auditor shall be appointed at the AGM who shall not be a member of the Committee.

Volunteers, including Officers and Committee members, shall be entitled to claim reasonable out-of-pocket expenses on terms approved by the AGM. No other payments shall be made to any members of the Group.

8. Amendments The constitution may be amended by a two-thirds majority of members present at an AGM providing that notice of the proposed amendment(s) has been publicly displayed in the Parish for a minimum of 21 days prior to the AGM, and has been sent to all Committee members. No alteration or amendment shall be made to the objects clause effecting the Group's charitable status without the prior consent of the Charity Commissioners.

9. Dissolution In the event of a resolution to dissolve the Group any assets remaining after the satisfaction of all debts and liabilities shall be given or transferred to a charity or charities in the Parish having similar objects, or if effect cannot be given to this provision then to any other charitable purpose agreed by a general meeting.

10. Rule A copy of this constitution shall be available to all members.

Note: This model is adapted from Ashill Village Aid and LINK - Box, Colerne and Rudloe Branch.

Appendix E

Good Neighbour schemes and 'community care'

Domiciliary health and social care (community care) services have been a concern of health and social services authorities and voluntary organisations for many years. The Government has given them particular priority since the 1980s. This resulted from a report from the Audit Commission which highlighted the unsatisfactory nature of many of the services that existed and demanded improvement.

A report, *Agenda for Action*, was commissioned from Sir Roy Griffiths and the Government considered his recommendations very carefully. The Government's own proposals are set out in the White Paper *Caring for People: Community care in the next decade and beyond*, and have become law in the NHS and Community Care Act 1990. The community care sections of the Act will be phased in by April 1993.

In the new proposals, Social Services Authorities will become responsible for ensuring that people in need of social care receive an appropriate 'package of care'. The Government's main aim is "to enable people to live as normal a life as possible in their own homes or in a homely environment in the community".

If the aims are to be realised, local people will need access to a wide range of services, from low-key 'good neighbourliness' to 24-hour specialised help.

Good Neighbour schemes such as those described in this guide can have an important role in community care. They offer friendly, flexible services to people who are beginning to need help to keep going but are not yet in need of 'the big guns'. They are an important addition to services such as the home help service, but cannot replace it or undertake more specialised care.

Appendix F

Glossary

ACRE

Represents Action with Communities in Rural England - national charity which supports the work of Rural Community Councils, including community development, information and advice.

CARER

Somebody who provides care to a person in need, often in that person's home. May be family, friend or neighbour. Many carers are themselves retired and living with the person for whom they care. Some carers may receive an attendance allowance.

CHARITY

A non-profit-making organisation assisting in the relief of poverty or providing education or housing for those on below-average incomes. Attracts tax and rating concessions. Subject to scrutiny by the Charity Commissioners.

CAB - CITIZENS' ADVICE BUREAU

A free volunteer-run personal advice service provided by over 1,000 branches throughout the UK.

CLIENT

A person who receives help. Some 'clients' may also give service as 'volunteers' in another capacity.

COMMUNITY CARE

Originally used to describe broadly-based good neighbour schemes (see below). It is now used to describe the provision of day care and other support services which enable people with special needs to stay in their own homes, rather than be cared for in institutions.

CRUSE — A national organisation with 185 branches in the UK that offers help to the bereaved, including counselling, practical advice and opportunities for social contact.

GOOD NEIGHBOUR SCHEME — Organised means by which local residents increase the amount of help given to one another. Matches potential volunteers with those in need.

GRIFFITHS REPORT — A Report which led to the Government White Paper *Caring for People*. This outlines a redirection of resources away from institutional care (eg hospitals, nursing homes, etc.) to Community Care, including domiciliary support services.

HOME HELP — A care assistant employed by Social Services who may do housework, cleaning, cooking, shopping, etc. for a 'client'.

HOUSING ASSOCIATION — A non-profit-making organisation which provides housing for rent and/or shared ownership, normally registered with the Housing Corporation.

JOINT FUNDING — Cash provided jointly by social services and health authority.

PARISH COUNCIL — The most local form of democracy, providing some local services and taking an active part in representing local opinion.

PATCH — Delivery of social services on a relatively localised basis with the stress on general rather than specialist help.

RCC — Rural Community Council - county-based charity which supports community development work, including work by parish councils.

Appendix F

Glossary

RDC	Rural Development Commission - the Government's rural development agency, which helps to encourage jobs and provides grant aid to local community projects in areas with a population of less than 10,000.
SHELTERED HOUSING	A housing scheme in which elderly tenants have their own self-contained accommodation but have a warden on call to provide help and emergency cover.
SOCIAL CAR SCHEME	Local service in which volunteer drivers provide pre-arranged lifts (normally door-to-door) to the doctor's, hospital, etc., or sometimes shopping trips, etc.
SOCIAL SERVICES	The local authority department which employs professional social workers and care assistants.
STREET (or ROAD) WARDEN SCHEME	A scheme in which volunteers are appointed to look after a street or block of houses, particularly to keep an eye on vulnerable residents, and provide quick response in times of need.
VILLAGE APPRAISAL	A local survey of public opinion and ideas for ways of improving community facilities and life.
VOLUNTARY ORGANISATION	Independent, non-profit-making, non-governmental organisation, probably involving volunteers, though may have some paid staff. Many are also charities.
VOLUNTEER	Someone giving help in an unpaid but often highly skilled capacity.
VOLUNTEER BUREAU	Local organisation which helps to recruit and place volunteers, and more generally promotes voluntary activity.